Table of Contents

Chapter 1: About the Online Industry

Chapter 2: Before You Get Started

Chapter 3: Getting Started

Chapter 4: Basic Writers

Chapter 5: Premium Writers

Chapter 6: Elite Writers

Chapter 7: Elite Plus Writers

Chapter 8: Other Ways to Make Money with iWriter

Chapter 9: Tips and Tricks for iWriter

Chapter 10: Making Money with Fiverr

Chapter 11: Making Money with Freelancer

Chapter 12: Commit to What You Do

Chapter 13: Shifting to Passive Income

Other Books By Ryan Stevens

Your Gift

Write a Review

Conclusion

Chapter 1: About the Online Industry

"The best time to plant a tree was 20 years ago. The second best time is now." – **Chinese Proverb.**

Every year, there are 500-1,000 new millionaires around the globe, and 80% of them succeed because of online expansion.

I simply wouldn't have enough space and time to cover how many millionaires are out there because of online expansion, but I will name a few websites/platforms that transformed the owners into millionaires:

- Forbes
- Amazon
- eBay
- AWeber

- Google
- Facebook
- Twitter
- Instagram
- Evernote
- GoDaddy
- Bluehost
- WordPress
- Ubisoft
- Blizzard Entertainment
- Udemy
- ClickBank
- BookBub
- Microsoft
- Flippa
- Freelancer
- Upwork
- 99designs
- Shutterstock
- Fotolia
- Fiverr
- Etc.

Should I mention that most of the companies above are actually making billions, not millions? There are millionaires in this world who made a fortune from selling mobile applications, books, websites, songs, etc. All of these sold online.

There are businesses that you haven't heard of yet and that I haven't heard of either.

Every year, more and more people are shifting from purchasing things from physical stores to purchasing on online stores and the reasons are obvious – it's faster, more comfortable, and you can buy multiple items at the same time.

What's even more interesting is that there are only 2 billion people who are connected to the Internet – the rest of the population is restricted (China, North Korea, Mongolia, etc.), poor (Africa, South America), primitive, or they simply don't care. However, the good news is that this number is constantly growing – technology becomes cheaper day by day and it grows, it expands. Obviously, the number of people who will buy things online will undoubtedly grow.

The whole process of gaining success in the online industry can be summed up in 3 simple steps:

1. *Come up with an idea.*
2. *Take action and commit to it.*
3. *Help others.*

Before we get into the 'meat', I want to show you why it's great to start an online business and then I will show you what to do to get started, even if you don't have any money to invest right now.

Chapter 2: Before You Get Started

It's so frustrating to see so many people being successful while we sit comfortably in our sofas, watching TV or wasting time, right? The truth is, most of the businesses require an initial capital, a background, a savings account, or something that can help you out.

You are probably sick and tired of seeing people running successful businesses and you simply wonder how they did it. Eventually, you will end up thinking that they did some sort of scam or they were just lucky.

The truth is that all of the successful people have several things in common: They work hard on a daily basis, they don't give up, they always find a solution when things go wrong, they always look for new ways to improve themselves, and they constantly invest their money.

Today, all those "requirements" to succeed can be easily converted into one single fact: You can win this game only if you want to. That's right, you can achieve anything you want, as long as you *really* want to.

20-30 years ago, it was harder and easier at the same time. The population was nearly half than it is today, but we didn't have access to modern technologies like mobile phones, Internet, digital content, etc.

With so much information right at our fingertips, I am seriously starting to stop feeling bad for those who don't do something for themselves with it. I was aware of the potential of the Internet since I was 18 years old, when I bought things from eBay and sold them locally (in Romania). At 19-20 years old, I started to write articles as a freelancer and I was making enough money to afford a new phone, a new laptop, gas for my car, and clothes from stores. As my parents were financially supporting me, $100-$200 extra every month was really helpful as a student.

The whole idea here is that I wanted to grow, to expand, to make even more money, and without scamming anyone. I wanted (and I still want) to build my own business, platform, and industry that I can count on (long-term).

In this book, I will show you a couple of ways to make money online without having to know anything spectacular, without having a degree, and without having to invest any money. I am very confident that you knew about these ways, but didn't know how or where to apply it. I was in the exact position a few years ago and that's why I found this topic helpful for people who want to grow, to start a business, but don't have the financial possibilities.

Life is expensive and sometimes, it's brutal. The purpose of life is to make us happy and to leave something as a legacy to our successors, but sometimes, it gets wild and holds us back from fulfilling our dreams and our mission. Fortunately, it can be tamed.

The businesses that I run now require money to start, invest, learn, etc., but I wouldn't have succeeded without a few tricks that I will show you.

You know what they say, "Don't keep all your eggs in one basket", so what this means is that you should invest your money elsewhere and start your own business.

Making money passively is one of the best things you can do in the 21st century. Even if you still need to work on a daily basis and you're paid for results and not for the total time that you work, a passive (online) business can continue to bring you money while you sleep, while you are on vacation, or while you do anything else.

When you start working as a writer or as a freelancer, you are making money actively. What you need to do is that you have to move towards passive income streams.

Why?

More free time, you can go on vacations whenever you want, you can grow as much as you want, and you can work as much as you want, with who you want, when you want.

If you have a job and you're already making money online but you want even more, you should start something new, generally something related to digital content (videos, courses, eBooks, a blog, a YouTube channel, an affiliate marketing business, etc.).

Most startups require money, so to initially make money, start from the bottom. Use the information within this book and use the simplest method to make money online even today.

No investments are required, so stop wasting your time and take action *now*!

Chapter 3: Getting Started

Please, do me a favor. As soon as you finish reading the whole book (or just after reading this chapter), please start taking action!

One of the fastest and easiest ways to make money online is to work write articles, proofread documents, or work as a VA (virtual assistant).

To do this, you just need an average-advanced English level; so you can start making money even if you're not a native English speaker. If you're a native speaker, you can make even more money with professional articles, but keep in mind that grammar is very important.

There are 3 places where you can start doing this and I will present one of them in detail (the fastest one):

1. *iWriter*
2. *Fiverr*
3. *Freelancer or Upwork*

I worked as a VA (on Freelancer) for an Indian woman and I was managing a website and writing articles for it. I was paid by the number of words that I wrote, so I was charging her $3/500 words (mainly for articles) and I was averaging 2,000 words a day. At the time, $10-$12 was a lot of money for me, but things have changed a lot since then.

Not long ago, I found a website called iWriter (http://iWriter.com), which basically allows anyone to sign up and start writing articles. Websites like http://Freelancer.com or http://upwork.com require patience until someone chooses you to work for him/her.

On iWriter, you can choose from the list and get right into the meat. As you get positive reviews, your status will automatically upgrade and you will earn even more money. I will cover everything about iWriter in the next chapters.

Fiverr allows you to what you want as long as it can be considered a professional service. Proofreading and writing articles can be a great way to start building an online business. At first, you should charge a lot less than your competition to attract more customers and get more reviews and then slightly increase the price.

If you have enough time, you can proofread on Fiverr and write on iWriter. If it was up to me, I would have chosen iWriter because you can start faster, work more, earn more money, and you can upgrade your status fast.

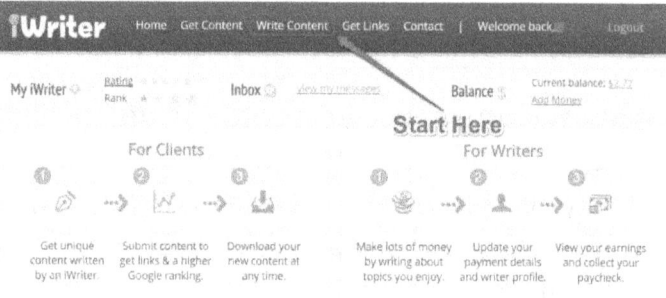

I worked on iWriter, so that's why I highly advise you to go there right now, create an account, attach your PayPal account or credit card, and get started.

What you should know before you start:

1. *Your articles can be rejected* – The hirer has the right to pay for the article only if he is satisfied with it.

2. *All your content will be automatically verified by CopyScape and you have to provide original content* – If you try to copy content from other sources, your account will be deleted.

3. *You have 3 hours to finish an article (on average).*

4. *If the hirer does not review your articles within 3 days (72 hours), your article will be auto-approved.*

5. *You are not allowed to give your personal information there (contact, email, Skype, etc.).*

6. You have to write clean content – You are not allowed to use any HTML formats.

7. Watch how many approvals (approval rate) the hirer has – A lower percentage means he/she has big standards and you might write an entire article and not be paid.

8. If the employers reject your work, they can give you a rating between 1 and 3 stars.

9. If the employer likes your work, but it needs some improvements, he can ask for a rewrite and you will have a limited time to finish that task.

Chapter 4: Basic Writers

When you start writing for the first time, you are a Basic (standard) Writer, so your earnings will be at the lowest levels.

As a standard writer, you will earn 1.25$/150 word article, 2$/300 word article, 3$/500 word article, 5$/700 word article, 7.5$/1,000 word article, 14$/1,000 word article. At all these rates you will have to pay a fee to iWriter.

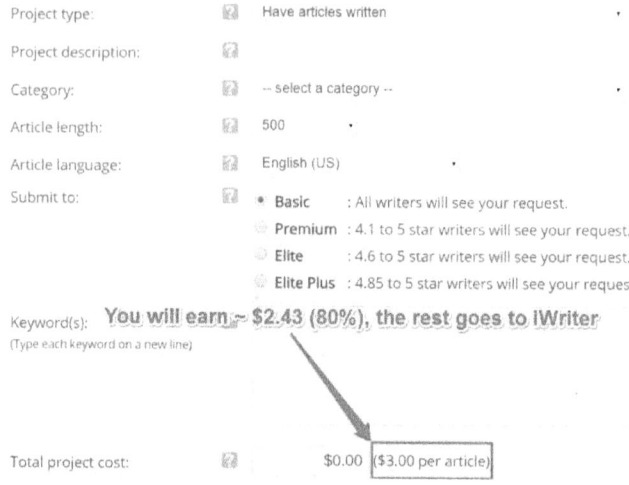

Project type:		Have articles written
Project description:		
Category:		-- select a category --
Article length:		500
Article language:		English (US)
Submit to:		• **Basic** : All writers will see your request.
		Premium : 4.1 to 5 star writers will see your request.
		Elite : 4.6 to 5 star writers will see your request.
		Elite Plus : 4.85 to 5 star writers will see your request.

Keyword(s): **You will earn ~ $2.43 (80%), the rest goes to iWriter**
(Type each keyword on a new line)

Total project cost: $0.00   ($3.00 per article)

So, your net earnings will be:

$1.01/150 words

$1.62/300 words

$2.43/500 words

$4.05/700 words

$6.08/1,000 words

$11.34/2,000 words

If you start writing articles today, for example, and you decide to write 5 articles/day at 500 words each, you will earn $2.43 x 5 = $12.15.

Most of the articles that are requested on iWriter are from 300 to 1,000 words, but rarely 2,000 or more.

Now let's take some examples:

In average, a 500 word article requires around 30-40 minutes to write. That means that if you work for 2 hours a day, you will be able to write 3-4 articles and you will earn, let's say, 4 x $2.43 = $9.72, which equals $291.6 if you work every day. If you work twice as much, you will earn $583.2 and if you work full-time, you could earn $1,166.4.

If you really need money, if you're a student, if you want to start a business but you need your money just to pay your expenses, then this sort of business can definitely supplement your needs. Things will get even more exciting when you surpass the Basic Level.

Unfortunately, you can't write an entire eBook, Kindle book, or rewrite other articles (bigger projects) unless you are at least a Premium Writer.

But here comes magic – you won't be a standard writer for too long (if you know English very well and don't make too many mistakes). You can quickly upgrade to Premium, Elite, or Elite Plus. You will continue to be a Basic Writer until you reach a minimum of 25 reviews and an overall rating of 4.1 or above.

Chapter 5: Premium Writers

Becoming a Premium Writer is easy if you work at least 4 hours a day. If you speak English proficiently and you don't make too many grammatical errors, people will rate you with 4 and 5 stars.

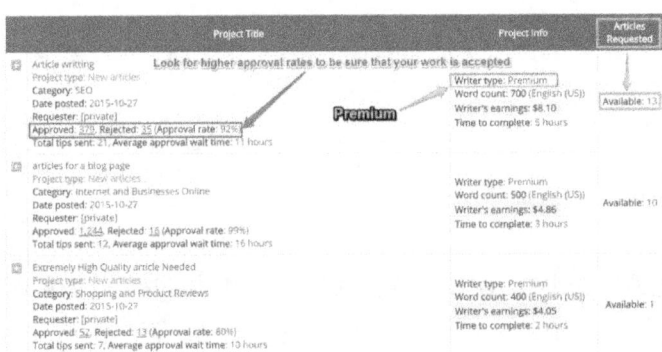

Premium writers earn more money than Basic Writers (almost double). Here are the rates (writer's net earnings):

$2.23/150 words

$3.65/300 words

$4.46/500 words

$5.79/700 words

$8.51/1,000 words

$24.31/2,000 words

Project type:	Have articles written	
Project description:		
Category:	-- select a category --	
Article length:	500	
Article language:	English (US)	
Submit to:	Basic	: All writers will see your request.
	Premium	: 4.1 to 5 star writers will see your request.
	Elite	: 4.6 to 5 star writers will see your request.
	Elite Plus	: 4.85 to 5 star writers will see your request.
Price per article:	$0.00 (minimum $5.50 per article)	

As a Premium Writer, you have a lot of advantages. You earn more, you can write eBooks, Kindle books, or even re-write articles.

The rates for writing books are also attractive:

$160 ($134.4 net) for 7,000 words ~ 20 pages

$275 ($231 net) for 12,250 words ~ 35 pages

$395 ($331.8 net) for 17,500 words ~ 50 pages

$590 ($495.6 net) for 26,250 words ~ 75 pages

$790 ($663.6 net) for 35,000 words ~ 100 pages

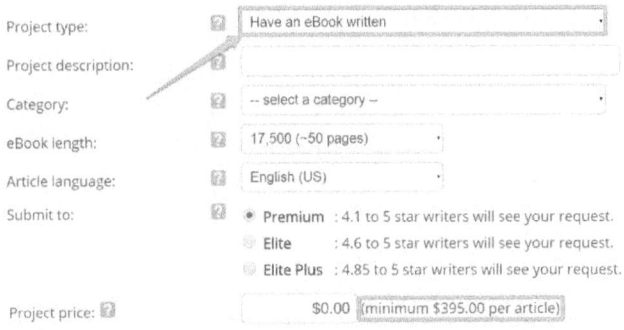

Now let's take the same example from the previous chapter – If you work for 2 hours a day (equivalent to 4 articles of

500 words), you will earn $4.46 x 4 = $17.84 a day. So, in 30 days, you will be able to earn up to $535.2 just by working 2 hours on a daily basis.

If you work 4 hours, this will transform into $1,070.4 and if you work full-time, you will be able to earn $2,140.8.

Let's assume that you will take some breaks or you will not work every day, and you can still make $500-$1,000 as a Premium Writer.

Chapter 6: Elite Writers

As an Elite Writer, you earn more than a Premium Writer and a lot more than a Standard Writer.

To become an Elite Writer, you need 30 individual reviews and an overall rating of 4.6/5 Stars. You can achieve this really quickly if you write 4-5 articles a day. It takes just a few days since you have become a Premium Writer, but to become an Elite isn't about the number of reviews, it's about the quality of the reviews. You have to make sure that the content is really good, almost perfect, to receive reviews of 4, 4.5, and 5, but you will need 4.5 and 5 reviews to achieve that level.

	Project Title	Project Info	Articles Requested
☆	Title: "Pushing Tesla to the Limit" Project type: New articles Category: Automotive Date posted: 2015-10-26 Requester: [private] Approved: 120 Rejected: 6 (Approval rate: 96%) Total tips sent: 5. Average approval wait time: 20 hours	Writer type: Elite Word count: 400 (English (US)) Writer's earnings: $6.89 Time to complete: 2 hours	Available: 1
☆	(Requesting) 5 star quality researched and science backed informative articles in the health niche Project type: New articles Category: Health and Fitness Date posted: 2015-10-27 Requester: [private] Approved: 756, Rejected: 14 (Approval rate: 98%) Total tips sent: 232. Average approval wait time: 9 hours	Writer type: Elite Word count: 500 (English (US)) Writer's earnings: $12.15 Time to complete: 3 hours	Available: 2
☆	Title: "Do you really need to change your oil every 3000 miles?" Project type: New articles Category: Automotive Date posted: 2015-10-27 Requester: [private] Approved: 120 Rejected: 6 (Approval rate: 96%) Total tips sent: 5. Average approval wait time: 20 hours	Writer type: Elite Word count: 400 (English (US)) Writer's earnings: $6.89 Time to complete: 2 hours	Available: 1

The worst part as a writer or as a freelancer is getting a bad review from someone who doesn't care at all about your work or about the whole process. Some people give 1-2 star reviews without hesitation.

Imagine if you have 15 reviews of 4.5 stars, 5 reviews of 5 stars, and 9 reviews of 4 stars. You need just 1-2 more reviews of 4.5 or 5 stars. For these reviews, your overall rating is (4.5 x 10 + 12 x 5 + 7 x 4) / 29 = 4.58/5

If you had 2 more reviews of 5 stars, your overall rating would be 4.61/5 stars (you will become an Elite Writer), but you meet a "nice" person who gives you a 1 star rating and you will drop to an overall rating of 4.48/5 and you will need to work even harder to achieve your initial goal.

If you receive too many negative reviews, your status can change quite fast, you can even lose your Premium Writer badge – sometimes, it could be your mistake, but sometimes… you just meet the wrong people.

Here are the rates: (Writer's net earnings)

$3.44/150 words

$5.67/300 words

$8.10/500 words

$10.13/700 words

$14.99/1,000 words

$33.2/2,000 words

Project type:	❓	Have articles written	▾
Project description:	❓		
Category:	❓	-- select a category --	▾
Article length:	❓	500 ▾	
Article language:	❓	English (US) ▾	
Submit to:	❓	**Basic** : All writers will see your request.	
		Premium : 4.1 to 5 star writers will see your request.	
		Elite : 4.6 to 5 star writers will see your request.	
		Elite Plus : 4.85 to 5 star writers will see your request.	
Price per article: ❓		$0.00 (minimum $10.00 per article)	
Keyword(s):	❓		
(Type each keyword on a new line)			

For the same example, if you write 2 hours a day (let's say 3 articles because it's harder to write), you will make $8.10 x 3 = $24.3, so in 30 days, this is equivalent to $729. If you work 4 hours a day, you can $1,458 and if you work full-time, you can earn $2,916. Assuming that you will work 4 – 8 hours a day 20-25 days a month will be equivalent to $1,000 - $1,500.

Writing eBooks or Kindle books will pay significantly more:

$210 ($176.4 net) for 7,000 words ~ 20 pages

$370 ($310.8 net) for 12,250 words ~ 35 pages

$525 ($441 net) for 17,500 words ~ 50 pages

$790 ($663.6 net) for 26,250 words ~ 75 pages

$1050 ($882 net) for 35,000 words ~ 100 pages

Generally, people rarely request full books, they usually request articles, but there are still some chances of finding such great offers of writing an entire eBook.

Chapter 7: Elite Plus Writers

This is the hardest status that you can achieve, but it has a lot to offer. If you manage to collect more than 40 individual reviews and you have an overall rating of 4.85/5 stars, then you become an Elite Plus Writer.

As an Elite Plus Writer, your earnings are 16 times larger than a Standard Writer's earnings. All you need to do is to get as many 5 star reviews as possible. Any other review will drop you down.

Here are the rates (Writer's net earnings):

$8.4/150 words

$15.12/300 words

$25.2/500 words

$31.5/700 words

$46.64/1,000 words

$92.4/2,000 words

Project type:	🔲	Have articles written	•
Project description:	🔲		
Category:	🔲	-- select a category --	•
Article length:	🔲	1000 •	
Article language:	🔲	English (US) •	
Submit to:	🔲	○ **Basic** : All writers will see your request.	
		Premium : 4.1 to 5 star writers will see your request.	
		○ **Elite** : 4.6 to 5 star writers will see your request.	
		● **Elite Plus** : 4.85 to 5 star writers will see your request.	
Price per article: 🔲		$0.00 (minimum $64.75 per article)	

If you have the opportunity to write an eBook as an Elite Plus, then you're gold. Here are the rates for eBooks or Kindle books:

$685 for 7,000 words ~ 20 pages

$1,195 for 12,250 words ~ 35 pages

$1,705 for 17,500 words ~ 50 pages

$2,560 for 26,250 words ~ 75 pages

$3,415 for 35,000 words ~ 100 pages

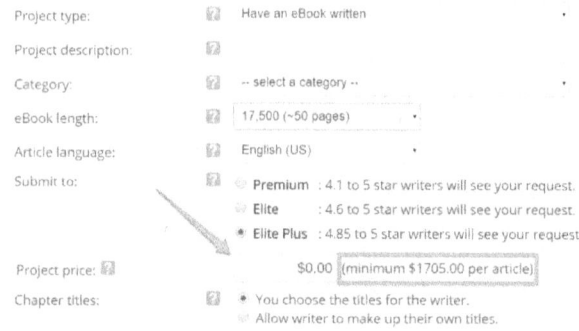

If you write 2 articles a day of 500 words (2 hours), you can earn up to $50 ($1,500 per month) net earnings, which is great. For 4 articles (4-5 hours), you get over $100 per day (or $3,000 per month) and for working full-time (25 days), you can expect $200 per day.

Now let's face it, it's extremely difficult to write 100% error-free articles as an Elite Plus, so you simply can't write more than 3,000 words a day (approximately $150) and you need a break from time to time. Anyway, you can still earn $3,000 a month as an Elite without a problem.

Chapter 8: Other Ways to Make Money with iWriter

I will show you how some users on iWriter make thousands of dollars in a legitimate way – they are Premium/Elite/Elite Plus writers, they take projects (extremely well paid), and they give them to basic writers. Of course, they need to 'polish' the basic content until it becomes truly professional, but there's a lot less work to do than starting from scratch.

Some basic writers are really good, but they don't have reviews and they don't have authority in front of others, so what they will do is to write for the lowest rates, so the 'smart' guys come in and take advantage of this scheme.

The same thing can be done not only with basic writers, but also with all the levels – an Elite outsources to a Premium or an Elite Plus to an Elite (or a Premium).

It's quite easy to spot the 'smart' guys – users get reviews only if they write content, so when someone requesting articles in the "Write Content" section has hundreds or thousands of reviews, it means that he's selling the content for profit.

Here are a few examples:

This method of making money with iWriter is profitable even if the Elites just proofread content from Premium Writers. The difference from Premium to Elite is double, and that difference is equivalent to 2 times more than a Basic Writer earns.

The 'polishing' is a lot faster than writing the whole article from the beginning.

Affiliate Program

As you would expect, every business/company has its own affiliate program.

iWriter has a great affiliate program that offers 50% of their profits.

Wait, wait... don't get too excited. You get 50% of their profits, which is around 20% of the total article. In other words, if an article costs $10 and iWriter would get $2, then you will get $1. So basically, you get 10% of the writer's earnings (who signs up to iWriter through your affiliate link).

The affiliate links can be put anywhere you have a big audience, such as Facebook (but not using Facebook ads), a blog, a website, etc.

Chapter 9: Tips and Tricks for iWriter

There are a few things that you may take into account when you are working on different articles. Here's a list of useful tips for writing, for iWriter, and for increasing your productivity.

- As a Standard Writer, write as many articles as possible to receive a Premium Writer status.

- To change your status quickly, write shorter articles – hunt the 150 word articles.

- Look for hirers with high approval rates – This way, you can avoid rejection.

- Avoid making too many grammar mistakes – You will easily get negative reviews and your overall rating will drop. It will become even harder to increase your rating.

- Write on topics that you are familiar with – If you like business topics or food topics or any other topics, write articles based on those. You will write faster and easier, and you will enjoy writing even more.

- As a Premium/Elite/Elite Plus Writer, hunt down eBook projects, they are a lot better paid than ordinary articles.

- Instead of writing new articles, go for rewriting articles based on a file, it's a lot faster and a lot easier.

- Write more than the hirer requests – This way, you will get maximum ratings, the hirer will add you to his favorite list, and you will have more chances to get more new projects, thus, more money.

- Avoid giving contact information via iWriter, as you can get warned or even flagged.

- Before starting to write, set up your PayPal account – Most of the payments (90%) will be made via PayPal.

- Always be grateful and respectful, write the articles on time, and follow the instructions carefully – You will increase your chances of being tipped.

- Look for hirers who tipped a lot of people (you will see their number of tips given) to get even more money.

- Schedule your time for writing – Schedule 2, 3, 5, 10 articles a day, how many you want, make a small calculation on how much money you want to earn.

- Make sure to sleep from 23:00 PM to 8:00 AM to have a maximum amount of energy – Don't stay awake until morning, you will be tired and won't be able to start working.

- Use a clepsydra or a timer (phone) to measure how much time you spend writing – This will help you improve yourself.

- Schedule a limited time for finishing one article and set a countdown timer – You will rush and work even harder and you will be a lot more focused when you will see that time is running out; you will be motivated to finish on time.

- Motivate yourself – Motivation is very important for anything in this life. Without it, you won't be able to do anything; immerse yourself, dream of what you want to achieve, how much money you want to earn, and after that, start working.

- Set goals – This is a very important aspect for improving yourself and keeping an eye on your progress.

- Improve your English and writing skills – Make no mistakes while you are writing articles, especially eBooks.

- Watch writing courses for different techniques used for fast typing, ghost writing, or academic writing – Improve yourself.

- Don't withdraw money from PayPal at every payment that you get; they will charge you – Wait for a bigger amount to come into your account and set fixed dates for withdrawing money.

- Hire other writers or proofreaders for increased productivity and amount of money (check previous chapter).

- Don't get distracted while you are writing. You will lose your ideas and it will be hard to keep the line going.

- Have a break occasionally – If you go on writing every day for hours, you will lose your imagination and productivity. Having a short break every week should be indicated.

- Be perseverant – This is probably the most important aspect of all.

Chapter 10: Making Money with Fiverr

Fiverr has something in common with iWriter – it allows you to make money online even when you don't have a dime!

The name, Fiverr, originally came from the price of the services, starting from $5, and they use 5 as a multiple ($5, $10, etc.) and it has great success in the online market.

Unlike iWriter, you can do almost anything; the possibilities are endless on Fiverr. Here is a list of what you can do and what you will find on the website:

- Proofread documents
- Write articles
- Create jingles
- Create songs
- Create voiceovers
- Edit audio files
- Edit videos
- Photo manipulation (Adobe Photoshop)
- Create covers (for eBooks)
- Create illustrations
- Code websites
- Design logos
- Design websites
- SEO
- Coaching
- Online marketing
- Advertising
- Create animations
- Create movies
- Translate documents
- Write stories for children's books
- Creating intros
- Etc.

Most of these mentioned above require skill, experience, and dedication, but some of them can be done just by mastering the English language, like proofreading documents, editing documents or writing articles (similar to iWriter). I suppose that if you are reading this book, you are capable of writing a few articles.

Levels on Fiverr

- *New Seller*
- *Level 1*
- *Level 2*
- *Rockstar (Top Rated seller)*

When you start on Fiverr, you don't have a status at all, but as soon as you fulfill a few requirements, you will upgrade to a Level 1 seller:

✓ *30 days active on Fiverr*
✓ *Complete at least 10 orders*
✓ *Maintain a +4 overall rating*
✓ *Keep a low cancellation rate*

Level 1 to Level 2 requirements:

- ✓ *Complete over 50 orders in 2 consecutive months*
- ✓ *Maintain a 4.5 rating or above*
- ✓ *Keep a low cancellation rate*

Level 2 to Top Rated Seller

- ✓ *Maintain a 4.7-5 star rating*
- ✓ *High volume of sales*
- ✓ *Low cancellation rates*
- ✓ *Exceptional customer care*

I personally don't look at 'Top Rated gigs' as they're the most expensive and they simply have too many offers and sometimes they rush things or it takes too much time to accomplish.

I talked previously about proofreading, which can be done just by mastering English (grammar, punctuation, etc.) and all the writers, publishers, authors, etc., need one (including me).

I personally use this gig (Outlawsphinx) as my main proofreader – She's doing an excellent job – great price, great service, great communication, a great person to cooperate with. Most of my documents and books (including this one) have been proofread and edited by her.

Outlawsphinx
Level 2 Seller

Now, I'll be completely honest with you – It takes a while to you get your first reviews, your first customers, and until you make your first pennies.

It's challenging, a lot more challenging than iWriter, but it can be done. Fiverr is great because it allows you to grow and expand and even create new gigs.

It takes a while until you reach your first 100 customers and 100 reviews, and then everything skyrockets by itself.

Unfortunately, people do illegal things on Fiverr, things such as selling fake reviews for products, books, courses, or other similar activities.

There were more than 1,000 people who were pursuing this on Fiverr and Amazon took action by sending all of them to court for violating their terms of service.

So, avoid doing such activities and focus on something legit and that you can grow by yourself.

Writing, editing, or proofreading articles is easy, legit, but it's competitive, so you'll need patience at first.

Fiverr can also be used as a self-promotional tool, too. For example, if you create a course on Udemy or you sell a book, you can 'sell' coupons on Fiverr with a 20% discount for who finds you there.

As you won't make too much money from this, it's a great tool to promote your products or services.

Chapter 11: Making Money with Freelancer

Another great place to start making money online (this is the place where I initially started) is http://Freelancer.com

The website is huge, the competition is high, but there're a lot of 'jobs' out there.

Assuming that you don't have any money, you can write articles, re-write articles, proofread documents, translate (if you know another foreign language), or you can become a virtual assistant.

It takes a while until someone picks you up, but you will eventually end up working for someone who is willing to work with you.

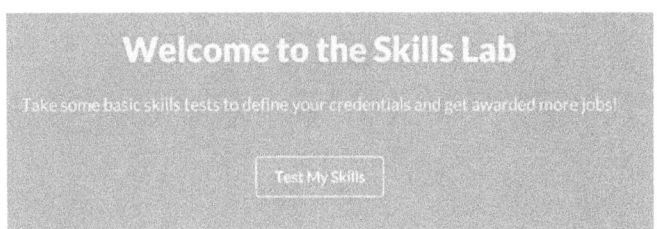

Fortunately, Freelancer allows users to get 'Licensed' in what they do – you can get a Freelancer degree in English (UK), English (US), Italian, French, Spanish, and other foreign languages, in mathematics, coding, web design, academic writing, Photoshop, Illustrator, After Effects, Google Drive, HTML5, translating from one language to another, and much, much more.

Each of these certifications costs only $5, so if you're willing to write high quality articles, you should be able to obtain a Level 2 or Level 3 (advanced grammar knowledge required) in English (which will cost $10-$15).

US English

LEVEL 1   LEVEL 2   LEVEL 3

Let's get to the numbers – While I was working a few hours a day for an Indian Automotive Forum back in 2012, I was being paid $3/500 words and I was averaging 2,000 words a day. I wasn't making too much money, but as a student, it was more than enough to cover a few expenses or to buy new things.

As a virtual assistant, you can earn $2-$5/hour and you can work from 2 to 8 hours, depending on the employer's requirements. On average, you should expect the lowest rates at the beginning and in those circumstances, you should make around $200-$300/month.

If you are just willing to write articles, then go to iWriter, it's faster and more profitable than this platform.

Chapter 12: Commit to What You Do

"If you can dream it, you can do it." - **Walt Disney**

It's easy to start doing something, it's easy to get excited about something you think you might be capable of doing, but the real question is *can you commit to it?*

People often tend to "dabble" things they do, they start doing something, they don't like the actual results, and they move to the next "thing". And the whole process repeats and over again.

One thing that I learned in my life (even though I am young) is that whatever you do, or whatever you want to do, it can be done only if you commit to it.

When I say "commit", I am saying that you need to be almost obsessed with your dreams and goals, you need to take action on a daily basis, to work, to struggle without stopping, until you reach your goals.

Goals don't need to be *big*, but you need to start slow by taking small steps. The more steps that you take (daily), the closer you'll be to your main goal.

When you commit to something, you need to give up on a few habits, such as going out every night, having fun all the time, procrastinating different activities, sleeping too much, or feeling sorry for yourself. Don't waste your time and start chasing your dreams.

Our goals are sometimes too big at first and we feel like we can't do anything about them or we need money to get everything started.

The whole point is that you can do something if you really want to reach what you want. This is the whole purpose of this book – If you want something big, start by doing something simple to make a few pennies.

The methods presented in this book are not rocket science, the websites/platforms that I presented will help you start your journey, but it's totally up to you how you do it and what you do after.

If you feel like you're making enough money from writing articles as a freelancer and you're happy with that, congratulations!

Just remember that you can do a lot more than that.

Chapter 13: Shifting to Passive Income

Freelancing is a great thing to do these days, it literally allows you to work even if you're in an airplane, on vacation, or anywhere else. It gives you flexibility, more free time, and the freedom to work with who you want.

Things can get even better than that.

Working as a freelancer is great, especially at the beginning or when you're used to working physically for someone else, but at some point, you'll want more than that.

While you work actively, start a business that will bring you money on the long-term (a passive income stream).

In other words, start shifting yourself from a freelancer to an entrepreneur.

If you are asking yourself, "What can I do to make money passively?", the answer is 'unlimited ways'. That's right, all you need to do is find the right niche or business that you enjoy doing.

One of the key features of all the successful online businesses is to start a blog or a website. There, you will build strong connections with people who love what you do and over the long-term, those relationships will convert to money, especially if you put a lot of value into them.

Here are a few examples of passive income:

- *Create e-courses*
- *Create eBooks*
- *Create an affiliate marketing business*
- *Start an Amazon FBA business*

- *Rent a property*
- *Start a YouTube channel*
- *Start a blog*
- *Build an email list and start selling products*

Passive income is great for those who want to be in full control of their business, who want to travel, who want free time, and who are capable of working at least 8 hours a day without being disturbed.

I've seen books and posts in which it was written that you can build a 7 figure business just by working 4 hours a week or 3 days a week. I don't believe those facts, especially the first one. I believe in daily action.

*"The secret of your future is hidden in your daily routine." – **Mike Murdock***

It's hard to keep up with multiple businesses, especially if you want to do them by yourself, but here's the truth: You can't to everything by yourself. You need to outsource what you can, to hire other freelancers to do the simple tasks that consume your precious time.

Your Gift

As a way of saying *thanks* for purchasing and reading this book, I am giving you a free gift and I invite you to take a look at my blog – http://entrepreneurenhanced.com

*To get this gift click on the photo or click on the blog to sign up to my email list.

**The gift is available starting with 20th November 2015.

Other Books By Ryan Stevens

Amazon Associates Affiliate Program

Learn the basics of affiliate marketing, and learn how Amazon Associates works.

Evernote in 90 Minutes or Less

Organize and de-clutter your daily tasks by installing this free app. A complete tour of the application is included and it's great for beginners.

Kindle Publishing PRO

Learn everything about Kindle Publishing from A to Z – How to upload, how to market, how to write, tips, tricks, and more.

Entrepreneur Enhanced

Learn the fundamentals of entrepreneurship and how I managed to start my own business. Strategies, experiences, and my own thoughts are all included.

CreateSpace Publishing for Independent Self-Publishers

Increase your income from self-publishing by creating print editions of your books. The whole process is free.

Express Book Launch

The unofficial guide for helping authors understand the process to perfectly launch their books.

Write a Review

I need your help.

I would really appreciate if you could write a short, descriptive review with all your thoughts about this book. Simply let me know if you liked or disliked it or share what you would you like to know more about in the review section.

Conclusion

Making money shouldn't be that hard these days now that we live in the 21st century where technology continues to explode. Earning money online should be part of our lives, even if we pursue other activities in parallel.

Thank you once again for taking the time to read this book.

Feel free to subscribe to my email newsletter to receive new offers or high quality books for the price of a cup of coffee (free or $0.99 books).

Regards,
Ryan